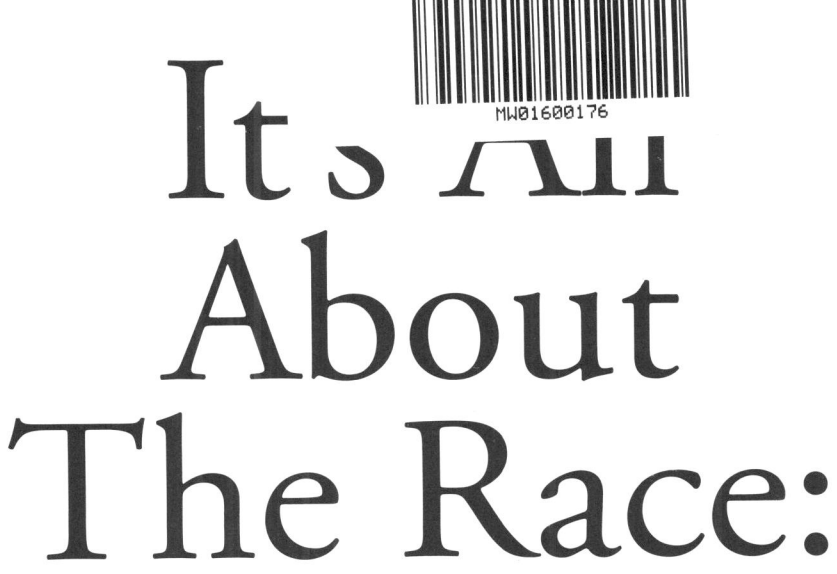

It's All About The Race:

Four Perspectives For Success

Written By

HENRY O. LAMAR, JR.

JAMES E. ROGERS, JR. ESQ

MURIEL D. WHORLEY

PETER CHARLES

Published & distributed by:
Henry O. Lamar, Jr.
James E. Rogers, Jr. ESQ
Muriel D. Whorley
Peter Charles

in association with:
IBJ Book Publishing
A division of IBJ Media
41 E. Washington St., Suite 200
Indianapolis, IN 46204
www.ibjbp.com

Cover design by D. Myntia Daniels.

ISBN 978-1-934922-44-6
First Edition

Library of Congress Control Number: 2011926367

Printed in the United States of America

Table of Contents

Foreword

———————————————————•———————————————————

THERE HAVE BEEN MANY textbook messages and theories about leadership and how to be a success; how to make things work, from effective leadership to culturally diverse leadership. Many bring a different spin to an old and weathered topic. But it all seems to boil down to one common denominator and that is utilizing good old-fashioned common sense for the situation at hand.

Our story is how to survive when faced with the challenges and barriers of being a minority in a non-minority dominated business race.

During the development of this "pocket" book, the four of us acknowledged the myriad of degrees of exposure we'd faced ranging from angst and concern to optimism, a renewed sense of freedom and ... well you get the point. Our experiences are intended to expose you to common hurdles in business life. It is not exhaustive and the book is not fictional, with a fairy tale ending. This work simply documents challenges we faced, and continue to face, and the tools or lessons used to overcome those challenges. We hope it serves to help equip you to manage in a national and global business race.

Collaboration on this book was driven by a collective sense of futility and vulnerability. We work hard, enjoy exemplary business success, and tout the corporate line; so, why can we become outcasts or ***persona non grata***? This book is a glimpse into our psyche and a lesson on how to endure the battle.

Our writings are influenced by recent history—never in our lifetime did we expect to see the gender and culture of the U.S. presidential candidates that we saw in 2008. Who would have dared dreamed we would have an African-American U.S. President in 2009? These events opened our eyes to untold possibilities and made us realize that the only limits that we face are the ones we place upon ourselves and guess what?

We can make our dreams come true and so can you. We want to; no, we need to pass the baton for others to continue the race because it is with perseverance, hard work, professional ethics and integrity that we will continue to maintain and support our culture and give our children and grandchildren the legacy they so rightly deserve.

Challenges for African-Americans in the Workplace

MURIEL D. WHORLEY

IMAGINE A WORLD WITHOUT discrimination, racism, insensitivity or retaliation. You are not imagining yourself in this environment in this day and time. You are dreaming of a reality that doesn't exist. Society uses all of the buzz words to ensure that the population believes that there **is** equity in the workplace. We hear "we do not tolerate discrimination," "X organization is an equal opportunity employer," "you are evaluated based on merit," or "pay for performance" and we are deceived into thinking that we will be treated as an equal in the workplace.

It doesn't take long to realize that we have left a university or campus environment and taken a leap of faith into a reality that doesn't exist. We thought that hard work and dedication would lay a foundation for our career—a career that could not be destroyed. What was our mistake?— we didn't factor "people" into the equation.

(Scenario One) Karen, a 22-year-old African-American, graduated from ABC University, magna cum laude, armed with multiple honors, a dedicated spirit, and the will to succeed. Karen goes on an interview with a government agency, convinced she is going to make her mark in the world. What could go wrong? She's a proven commodity and she has the evidence in her portfolio. Karen attends the interview, suitably impresses her interviewers and lands a job as an entry-level analyst. Of course, she passes all of the required security checks and she eagerly begins work on the following Monday.

1

It doesn't take Karen long to realize that she is given the assignments lacking in visibility or exposure—in essence no one else wants them. However, that doesn't diminish her enthusiasm for a job well done until she realizes that most of her products are shelved. What can she do to make an impact? How does she approach management to let them know that she is capable of so much more?

(Scenario Two) Sam is a 21 year-old applicant of African-American descent, who has multiple degrees in accounting. He is also a Master Public Accountant. Sam is tri-lingual, which is a competency that is sorely needed in today's multi-cultural environment. Unfortunately, he doesn't have any actual experience in the workplace. Sam lands a position at a private corporation as a junior accountant. He is immediately assigned to assist John, one of the corporation's senior accountants. Sam brings organizational skills to the position and a strong desire to succeed. John recognizes ability and competency in Sam and, in a manner that suggests confidentiality, advises Sam that he is going to allow him to make a major contribution to a high-level project that has been assigned to John. Sam naively assumes that this is the foothold he needs to prove his value to the corporation. Sam approaches the task with confidence in his abilities and is not proven wrong. Unfortunately, when it came time to present the results at a meeting with both his and John's executives, Sam was not in attendance nor was his contribution attributed to him.

Sam is disappointed and unsure of next steps. He doesn't want to upset the applecart by voicing his displeasure but neither does he want his significant contribution to the project to go unnoticed. What are Sam's options?

Unfortunately, these scenarios happen routinely to African-Americans in the workplace. In order to pinpoint the problem, we need to look at the root cause. So often, African-Americans have been brainwashed into believing any opportunity presented to them is a gift and should be treated as such. We should thank the donor and be forever in their debt. We should express our gratitude by continuing along a course of action that assures the donor that we are aware that the debt will never be repaid. We have not mastered the art of believing in ourselves and working as a cohesive population intent upon expressing that we bring a value to the situation that would be missing if we were missing. We need to realize our worth, and capitalize on the very real fact that many of our accomplishments are needed and would not have otherwise been realized. In addition, we have been deceived into thinking that we are unable to make significant contributions without the help of others and if we get too sure of ourselves, we are reminded that we are not in control.

(Scenario 3) Bob achieved a level of organizational leadership that had been unheard of before he took over the reigns as the Chief Administrator for a large hospital. Bob was aware that racism was alive and well but it had not impacted him, therefore the problem must lie elsewhere.

His executives had always treated him with respect, recognized his abilities, rewarded his accomplishments, and valued his ideas. So if they didn't value the ideas or accomplishments of other African-Americans—the problem must be with the other African-Americans. Bob was a witness to the fact that his executives were fair-minded—after all look at where he is today. Sure, he has seen glimpses of inequality throughout the years but, hey, they must have deserved it—it could not be racism or biased behavior. As a matter of fact, just yesterday, Michael, an African-American manager in radiology had submitted a best practice idea that actually had a lot of merit. The hospital board told Michael that while the concept was good, the research, the follow-through and the hypotheses were weak. The board advised Michael that if he were to ever go further in the organization he needed to enhance his skill sets or resign himself to remaining in his current position. Bob didn't agree, he thought the report was well thought-out, well-researched and would save the hospital millions if implemented. Bob did not speak up nor show his support of Michael. Why? Because his judgment may be called into question and he valued his position. Besides, no one helped him get to where he was, and if the board had serious reservations about Michael's report there certainly must be good reason. Bob took one look at Michael's face as he exited the room and clearly saw the words "sell-out" blinking in neon lights. Bob had let a colleague down, but he had to, he needed this job and he valued his authority.

This is another scenario that African-Americans face on a daily basis. Why? Because we do not currently have a strong foothold among society's elite and we unfortunately equate money with power, therefore, we believe that the only way to achieve greatness is through financial achievements.

That is a far cry from the truth; we should equate knowledge with power and richness with health, integrity, morality, fairness and equity. We need to value our families and nurture our religious beliefs. We need to focus on obtaining an education and educating others as opposed to striving to be accepted by people we don't even respect. Once we realize our value, and focus on our goals, we will truly realize that the challenges we face on a daily basis are not insurmountable, merely stumbling blocks that can be overcome by diligence, confidence, fortitude, strength of character, and the ability to realize your personal shortcomings, make them your strengths and, at the opportune time and in a professional manner, vocalize your value.

Being the Only One

HENRY O. LAMAR, JR.

THIS ARTICLE IS ABOUT being the only African-American in an organization or a work group in any public or private company. It also addresses strategies and techniques to cope with this potentially stressful situation.

I spent the first 24 years of my life in a Black world—the segregated communities and schools of Macon, Georgia and Fort Valley, Georgia. I have spent the past 34 years under very different circumstances. Upon graduation from high school, I attended and graduated from Fort Valley State College with a bachelor's degree in education, with a concentration in social science. I received a fellowship to attend the University of Georgia to pursue a Master of Public Administration (MPA) degree. There were few African-American students at the university and fewer still in public administration. Of the approximately 100 men in my residence hall, I was the only African-American. In my lecture classes, which included courses outside of the public administration discipline, all too often, I was "the only one." As an African-American, I was a stranger in a strange land.

The misfit was complete: socially, psychologically, and academically. The course demands of the public administration curriculum gave me little time to socialize within the small Black student community at school. I was also hampered by the fact that I went home to Macon every weekend. My social isolation and segregated experiences strained interactions on both sides in my dealings with Whites. I was cautious about interacting with Whites in any situation, social or educational, because of fear of reprisal or rejection. I felt that Whites were cautious because they either didn't know how to react to a Black man in "their" world or they were not sure how I would react. Of course, there were some Whites that didn't want me there and they expressed their views through stares, whispers and other non-verbal communication. There were, however, more Whites than I ever expected who greeted me with apparent open arms. My world, previously viewed in Black and White, was forced open and I began to learn about, accept, and enjoy other kinds of diversity among people. I found that exposure and interaction in living and learning environments could, for the most part, cure what years of separation had produced on both sides. My roommate Henry, who was White, became my friend and mentor. As a math major, he was able to help me successfully complete a Fortran computer language course. I was required to take this course, but my computer and math skills were lacking in some respects. Without Henry's assistance, I would not have passed the computer course and therefore would not have graduated on time with my MPA degree. My perspective on race relations changed dramatically because of my interaction with Henry. Not so much because he assisted me with a difficult class, but because I actually became friends with a White person.

My job search was a defining moment in my life. I was a product of and beneficiary of the civil rights movement. White America was very interested in hiring African-Americans to show their support of the civil rights struggle. Because of their desire to demonstrate equal employment opportunity, many companies seemed eager to hire me because of the color of my skin. I wanted a job to demonstrate my abilities but most of those who recruited me wanted a "statistic." Local community governments were offering me city manager positions and police department positions in small and medium sized towns across Georgia. The job offers were tempting because I wanted and needed a job badly. While the financial support that I received to pursue my graduate degree had covered most of my expenses, I still needed some financial assistance from my parents. I wanted to make my parents proud of me as well. I was determined, however, that the job I accepted would satisfy my personal hierarchy of needs, including a sense of value and an organizational belief in my abilities and capabilities. The job also had to add to my sense of pride and independence in making my career decision. I visited with several local governmental representatives and several representatives of local police departments before deciding that the jobs being offered were not meeting my needs. I then began to focus my attention on the federal government. Because I had graduated in the top ten percent of my class, I was placed, along with others similarly situated, at the top of agency recruitment certificates. I also passed the Federal Service Entrance Examination and received a very competitive ranking at the GS-5 and GS-7 levels. As a result, I was called for interviews before representatives of two government agencies. Before my first interview I was nervous, of course, but when I saw the members of the interview panel (two Whites and one African-American), my anxiety level diminished somewhat. I then recognized the African-American as the radio personality from my hometown. "Satellite Papa" was an extremely popular "D.J." and I felt confident that he would provide support during the interview. Man, was I ever wrong! He drilled me mercilessly while the other two panel members had very few questions for me. Needless to say, I did not get that job. I did, however, learn a valuable lesson that day – don't assume that being interviewed by a person with your racial background gains you any advantages. I let down my guard, assuming that everything would be all right because a popular African-American was on the interview panel. I learned my lesson and was much better prepared and more confident in my own abilities when representatives from another agency interviewed me. There were no African-American panel members and the White panel members were as tough as "Satellite Papa" had been. I applied what I had learned from my first interview to the next interview. I was offered a position as an Administrative Intern. This position afforded me the opportunity to have rotating assignments between the various administrative functions (Personnel, Training, Facilities Management, EEO, and Public Affairs). I accepted the position and became the first African-American Administrative Intern in the agency's Southeast Region. This was exciting and very challenging to me because I would be a pioneer. I felt that the position would meet my personal needs and I also perceived the work environment to be viable for significant personal contributions to the organization and for appropriate rewards for performance. The interviewers, their description of career opportunities with their agency, and printed recruitment materials all helped to make me feel good about my decision.

Making the transition from college to the working world is always difficult, but it's even more difficult when you are the only one of your kind (African-American). At offices that hire scores of college graduates every year, new employees go through training together, ask stupid questions together, and lament over their lowly status together. But when you are the only college graduate in your occupation and the only African-American, all the normal insecurities about starting a new job in the adult world feel like they're uniquely yours because you can't see anyone else going through the same thing. There was no one else like you available to talk with about issues you faced. Issues like dealing with jealousy and envy from African-Americans and Whites ("I've been here for years and I didn't get that opportunity," "I'm not going to help him with anything, they gave him the job, not me"), dealing with low expectations from superiors and peers alike ("they just hired him because of the color of his skin, he won't make it, he'll wash out just like the others, but they can say they gave him the opportunity"), dealing with the tremendous responsibility of being not just the "only one," but the "first one" as well.

If you're lucky, like I was in my first assignment after graduation from the intern program, you will have a compassionate boss who will offer reassurance and patience with basic questions. In between the time that you're hired and the time you find that compassionate boss, you must succeed by learning to be your own mental cheerleader. You cannot allow isolation to overwhelm you. If you begin the job thinking, "I'm the youngest person here," "I don't know what I'm doing," "these people don't like me"—if you go in feeling overwhelmed—you're not going to get anything accomplished. You have to say to yourself that if the experience is going to be a positive and beneficial one, I must take personal responsibility for my growth and development. During my three years of rotational assignments, I experienced the full range of emotions from fear and trepidation about being the only intern and the first African-American intern, to unspeakable joy over the experience I had obtained. My work experience covered such areas as writing internal management documents for the start-up of a new training facility, assisting in the design of work space at the new facility which also included administrative and operational components, serving as a recruiter, personnel specialist, training and development specialist, public affairs specialist, EEO specialist, just to name a few.

I experienced a sense of alienation at work at times feeling like an outsider looking in on the agency's network of colleagues. There were times when my co-workers appeared to look at everything they did through a filter of race and were sometimes unsympathetic to the minority point of view. Race only complicates the difficulties an African-American might already face in the workplace. Oftentimes, a White co-worker or boss is insensitive to feelings of their African-American colleagues. Sometimes they may be racist or hold strong prejudices. On the other hand, there was also the tendency by African-American employees to view every piece of feedback to them or any negative action taken against them as racist.

As I began to prove myself in the intern program, I gained acceptance and opportunities for more challenging assignments. In addition, upon graduation from the program my first permanent job assignment was with a wonderful, supportive supervisor who encouraged me personally and professionally.

Since that time, I have learned many lessons about being the only African-American in my work environment. The following are perhaps the most important:

- Don't expect to be loved or accepted as an insider, but give and expect respect. Some may still not like you, but if you demonstrate honesty and integrity in all of your actions, most will respect you.
- Do your job well; do not cut corners. It is always better to over-prepare by broadening your perspective beyond the issue at hand, think about how the next steps should be completed in your function as well as in other parts of the organization. In my case, it was true what my parents and others had told me about having to work twice as hard as Whites to be recognized. Learn what's important to your organization and work to fill that need. You must do your current job well in order to be considered for the next job in your career progression.
- Do not self-promote, but do expect honest recognition for your contributions. I'm sure you're aware of the adage, "If you don't toot your own horn, no one else will toot it for you." It's OK to extol

the virtues of your accomplishments, just make sure that you aren't the only one extolling.

- Dress appropriately for the company's culture, not yours. Honor your heritage but take into consideration the culture of your workplace. Is the dress code casual attire, business casual attire or business attire? It will most likely never be "anything goes." My view as a new employee and as an employee with over 30 years of service was that there was nothing casual about my business. I wore business attire at all times.
- As you do not wish to be judged by the color of your skin, do not judge others in that manner.
- Find your voice, but learn when to speak and when to hold your tongue. Holding your tongue can sometimes get you branded as "quiet and reserved." Even if you communicate as much as you need to and your communication is of high quality and substance, you may still be branded, but the brand won't be a fatal flaw for you in terms of career progression. Keep slang to a minimum.
- Attend the meeting before the meeting. Get there early. "Small talk" before the meeting is not for icebreakers. Power moves often take place before the session begins.
- Network, network, network. Give to others without keeping score. You will be amazed at the amount of valuable information and insight you can and will obtain if you talk to and with your colleagues.
- Attend office parties that occur during the workday and make arrangements to show up at a few after work or weekend gatherings. This will help dispel the idea of you being an outsider. A lot of team bonding occurs during happy hours, golf outings and cookouts. Despite the frivolity, stay focused and don't let your guard down.
- Find out who you are and work toward whom you want to be; do not delude yourself, but neither should you accept others' limited expectations of you.
- Expand your support structures—look to faith communities, sororities or fraternities, minority professional societies, service groups, housekeeping staff, and departmental secretaries. One of my mentors throughout my career was a member of the custodial staff in my first office. She began her mentoring of me when I

began my job as an Administrative Intern. She would speak with me every day and her words were always supportive and encouraging. I began my career in 1971. Even though I moved around the country between 1971 and 2005, whenever I was in Atlanta, we would always talk. She was a major inspiration to me and I was proud to recognize her at my retirement party.

- Learn how to learn and how to solve problems. Be flexible and make adjustments as appropriate.
- Don't jump the gun. Always step back and analyze your interactions with colleagues. In your mind, play back comments or incidents you find offensive to make sure you are not just reacting emotionally to them. Then weigh your options and make the appropriate decision.

Being the only one can place you on an emotional roller coaster if you are not grounded in knowledge, confidence, and the ability and desire to learn more. I knew that I could succeed in the business world. I just needed a chance to prove it. I was given that chance and, as they say, "the rest is history."

How to Get to Know the System

JAMES   E.   ROGERS,   JR.   ESQ

YEARS OF EDUCATION TO develop knowledge, skills, and expertise are critical to success in business. But many educational institutions fail to disclose that knowing the "system" and culture of an organization may be equally and/or more important than one's educational pedigree. Therefore, fresh new graduates and other new employees fail in organizations because they have been shortchanged in not being advised that formal education has its limits; that their education must be enhanced outside of the classroom to develop the skills to learn both the formal and informal systems of the business. Of course, one can learn critical information from various reports and business plans and even from internal operating procedures. But where do you learn how the business really operates, and how do you learn to master the system? The key is to get on the proper "networks!"

Cultural and systemic networks in business can be a challenge to conquer; however, there are several practices that are extremely helpful. Initially, try to spend time with your supervisor to get the lay of the land. Office and lunch times provide great opportunities to develop your relationships. I strongly suggest that you limit your "off the clock" interactions to office and/or business group activities that are attended by several or more members of the workforce. Limit private one-on-one time out of the office because of the possibility of conflicts of interest, uncomfortable situations, or becoming the unwanted subject of the office rumor-mill. In discussions with your supervisor and other members of the workforce, and through observation, find out several things:

1. Who are the formal and informal organizational leaders?
2. Who are considered the best secretaries and/or administrative personnel?
3. Who has been successful mentoring new hires throughout the organization?
4. What community activities does the business sincerely support and how can you become a part of the business' support of that activity even in your "off the clock" time?
5. Observe the work habits of the persons that are considered the "stars" within the business. Further decide which of their respective work habits you may wish to emulate.
6. Ask your supervisor if the business will allow shadowing opportunities. This is a great way to get to know the business as well as to establish professional relationships with key personnel throughout the business early in your tenure.
7. Get to know the janitorial staff! I am always amazed by the organizational knowledge of the janitorial staff and how their vast knowledge is consistently overlooked.
8. Explore ways to add each of the people referenced above to your library of resources.

Organizational systems are based on concepts of people who have successfully brought their ideas to the table to make the business successful and in so doing have created a culture that for the purposes of the business works. Every successful business has one, and the strength of the culture is sometimes reflective of the strength of the systems that support it. That is why real change at companies is made at the systems and cultural levels, not by simply changing the organizational structure.

To get to know the system and the culture of a business is extremely time and energy consuming. However, when you have mastered the culture and the system the sky is the limit for your success. To master the culture and the system puts you in a position to make informed decisions on many different levels that have both organizational and personal impact.

Some of the recommended contacts referenced above are very obvious, but two categories are probably surprising, those being administrative support and the janitors. How can these people in the "lowly" positions help you? The fact that you have this question is an indication that you have a lot to learn, and should be a further warning to you to review the value you put on people vs. position. The information that these people have is unbelievable! Administrative staff sees, hears, prepares, distributes, and reviews the vast majority of paperwork, presentations, budgets, and other key documents of the business. Simply put, everyone's secretary has more information than you have. In addition, managers and executives will often confide things to their administrative staff that they may not even confide in their spouses. The same is true for the janitorial staff. In many instances, these individuals walk in and out of meetings and offices totally ignored, but they hear and see everything. Further, almost like the family cook, many have relationships with executives and managers that allow them to discuss many personal issues regarding the business as well as family. A well placed word by one of these individuals may aid your career or hurt your career if your interactions with these individuals are negative. For example, I am aware of several leading executives that test potential candidates by having them wait in a waiting area for their respective interviews to watch their personal interactions. If during the period they are waiting they fail to positively engage in a conversation with the administrative staff and/or the janitorial staff they have lost the job before the interview. The reason for the "test" is simple, most managers and executives want to know how the potential employee generally treats people, especially those in the workplace. If the candidate comes across as arrogant and/or superior to the administrative support and the janitors, it is believed that the potential employee will come across that way to others regardless of status or position. Always value everyone at all times and it will help you accomplish your goals.

Make the Office
Games Work for You

PETER CHARLES

WHETHER ONE WORKS IN construction, in manu-
facturing or in an office environment, we have all seen it,
heard about it and likely been victim to it. What is *it*? It
is those inevitable office games that people play. Office games can be
played by almost anyone including colleagues and bosses with whom
we associate in the course of the day. Some are innocent bystanders or
pawns, while others are masterful play setters and action manipulators.
The true players, however, are those who recognize the games and make
them work toward the advancement of their careers.

So what do these games look like? They take many forms. A game
can be any misdirection, misrepresentation or well-placed rumor. It is
something you may not notice coming from others and subtly introduced
by others at a critical moment. It can have the intended or unintended
purpose of derailing the execution of a well-planned course of action.
How we handle these games sets the stage for how others view us and
how they believe we will react in similar situations. A failure to properly
react or rise to the occasion exposes weaknesses, or what I refer to as
buttons, that others may recognize and push at opportune moments to
diminish one's position while maximizing their own.

Cover your buttons. That is, know your weaknesses and make
them work to your advantage. We know our strengths; we accentuate
them, display them and look for opportunities to exploit them. But
our tendency is to ignore our weaknesses or insecurities. Unfortunately,

ignoring our own weaknesses doesn't stop others from observing and using them to their advantage. This is unconscionable. It is akin to providing the opponent in a sporting match a list of the techniques that you have not mastered. It is unconscionable because such exploitation is avoidable. It is a simple concept.

Consider the colleague that in nearly every way is your equal. She is talented, creative, proficient and articulate in the art of business. This person shines behind the scenes developing exceptional business proposals, but is insecure in presenting proposals because of an innate sense of inadequacy among peers and superiors. She is an introvert. You are also talented, creative, business savvy and you are quite the extrovert. Aside from the obvious, the difference between you and your colleague is your tendency for inattention to detail, while your colleague's focus is detail. In essence, you dazzle with charm while your colleague struggles to articulate brilliance. If you are the introvert, how do you cover this button?

One perspective is to acknowledge the shortcoming while ignoring it. I refer to this as the *teflon effect*. That is, know your inadequacy and celebrate it. How do you do this? Tell your audience about it. Explain why you're uncomfortable, why you feel inadequate and ill-prepared. Many will relate. Then, move on. Do your job and what you do best. In most cases, it is likely that it is the attention to detail that will dazzle. Find a place where you are comfortable and then exploit it. Ignore your inadequacies, because at this point everyone knows what they are and there is nothing to be exposed.

Anyone that does not feel a sense of inadequacy in some situations is in denial. Always acknowledge your shortcomings and accentuate your strengths. Recognizing both can help you rise above any office games with you as the target. When you know what you bring, for better or worse, the games are always in your favor.

Sharing for Credibility vs. Sharing Too Much

JAMES E. ROGERS, JR. ESQ

I N THE BUSINESS WORLD and in our personal lives one of the greatest challenges is to establish enough credibility to make the process and system work in our best interest. Many in business environments believe that doing a "great job" on a project will be sufficient to move one's career forward, or that an outstanding work product will influence those in charge to fully value the contributions of all involved. Those who fall prey to these misconceptions face a harsh reality once they hit the glass ceiling and find that doing a "great job" and maintaining "outstanding" performance is not enough. So what is it that gets you to the next level?

In any workplace the quality of performance is one key to success. In every situation you should give your best effort to achieve organizational objectives at the highest possible levels. However, performance is rarely enough simply because performance without the credibility of the performer fails to impress those with the power over one's career. This may sound strange but it happens every day. For example, how many times do you choose one product over another simply because of brand recognition? Is there really such a difference in soft drinks, laundry detergent, cars, and phone service that one is clearly superior to the other based on taste, and/or performance? Generally our decisions are made based on branding credibility, even if the other product is at a much lower cost.

The same process applies in the workplace. Have you ever been in a situation in which you clearly have the best idea or plan but the organization elects to follow the proposal of someone with a poorer plan and weaker idea? Many times, although race and gender may come into play, that decision is made based on the organizational and personal credibility of the presenter. To move forward in your career and business you want to be the person with that type of credibility. So if performance alone does not earn you this type of credibility, what does?

The key, in addition to performance, is sharing enough to build personal and business relationships. Sharing "*what*" you ask?! Sharing enough about yourself and your life that those you work with are "comfortable" with you. Even in this world of tremendous technology and instant communications, the rapport, that we establish is the key to success. This sharing takes place in meetings, telephone conversations, and even email. Let's discuss what to share, when to share, and how much to share.

When entering any relationship, whether business or personal, it is natural to want to know something about the person we are dealing with. We want to know if the person is ethical, trustworthy, dependable, and likeable. In business, I suggest that this sharing be at a very high level and limit the sharing to only the things you want to be public. For example, people are interested in whether you are married with children. If you are, these are great conversations that allow limited insight into your life. You can talk about your spouse and kids in generalities for hours if necessary, without revealing your personal thoughts and opinions. If single, choose your parents, siblings, nieces and nephews, but keep all conversations general without great detail. It is amazing, but with these conversations you can build a great deal of intimacy with people without revealing anything truly personal. Further, exceptional life experiences in college and/or the military will serve the same purpose as do the general topics of sports, the weather, and vacations. Avoid conversations concerning religion, race and politics unless there is a business purpose. The skill is to reveal what you can readily accept as being public, not private, information. Why? Because whatever you choose to share will become part of the "book" on you. Keep in mind that everyone has a "book" that parties share freely with each other. Many times after a presentation or an interactive meeting I have heard participants recapping the presentation and/or the discussion and quickly transition from talking about the subject matter to the "book" on the person. So it is important that you write your own "book" as much as possible.

Keep your book CLEAN!! There are things that you should never share in a business setting and with people you work with such as:

- Financial information or problems
- Problems with your spouse
- Problems with your children unless they have overcome a challenge in a positive manner
- Intimate details of your negative family history
- Anything that you do not want to be public

Take time to think about how you would like your "book" to read. Since you are the subject and author you are in control of the vast majority of its contents. Make sure that the "book" is positive and its contents are of the nature that others will have the desire to be associated with you. The positive aspects of the "book" combined with superior performance will aid you greatly.

A poor or negative book will have an equally negative impact on your ability to move forward. As people discuss your positive qualities they will also review your negative qualities. I have seen instances in which decision makers used personal issues to determine that a person with superior skills was not dependable and trustworthy enough for a promotion. When this negative train leaves the station it gains momentum quickly and picks up many passengers, especially those that may have been on the fence. Controversial financial decisions, marital issues, and other gossip quickly come to the forefront and become major talking points which obscure the positive attributes you bring to the table. You can be the subject of negative "spin doctors" and have your career destroyed before you ever know what hit you.

Write your "book" with the chapters, messages, and substance that you want to promote. Your life is your message—control your life and you will control your message.

Don't Burn (Out) Your Mentor

JAMES E. ROGERS, JR. ESQ

T HERE ARE A NUMBER of books and articles regarding the importance of mentors in one's career. Mentors play an invaluable role in directing us through organizations and various professional and personal situations. Mentors can be visible, but in many instances operate behind the scenes opening doors and opportunities with their advice or a simple well-timed word to the right person. There are several important guidelines that a mentee should follow to enhance the mentor/mentee relationship.

First, respect the confidence of the relationship! I have found that the best mentor/mentee relationships are those that are not public and both parties confide in the strictest manner. These discussions can be free and open with no concern of one party hurting another's feelings but most importantly that no one else will know about the conversation or the advice that was provided. This high level of confidence must be maintained whether the advice works or not. I have observed several instances over the years when the bonds of confidential conversations have been broken with dire consequences. In one instance, after confidential advice had been given, the mentee communicated her concerns in writing to the head of the office and in the text of the letter referred to her mentor by name as the source of the information she was sharing. In another instance, I observed a mentee at an after-work happy hour, tell his mentor's colleague (after too much to drink) what his mentor thought of his colleague. Both of these episodes ended the mentor/mentee relationship and the parties left their respective organizations under a cloud.

Only share information publicly when the mentor has specifically instructed you to do so, otherwise keep the information solely for personal use. Further, keep the name of your mentor private unless your mentor gives you specific permission to state your relationship. In these instances, if you have doubts about what can be publicly stated always err on the side of silence. If the wrong choice is made through silence, it may be generally corrected by another opportunity to share the information with the right party. However, once the information is public you can never call it back and it takes on a life of its own.

Second, if you value the advice act on it! Have you ever repeatedly provided advice to a person who never acts on it? It is extremely frustrating for your mentor to share his/her time only to have you appear not to value the advice. Even if you choose to do something different get back to your mentor and explain your choice. The mentor may not agree with your decision, but he/she will know that you valued their advice enough to be considered. This interaction may help to foster the relationship over a long period of time rather than the relationship potentially being short-lived.

Third, be a resource to your mentor. The mentor/mentee relationship should not be a one-way street only supporting the goals of the mentee. If you want to enhance the relationship with your mentor be prepared to assist him/her if the opportunity arises. Be aware that in some instances what may appear to be a simple request may be as much a test as it is a true need. Responding appropriately to the request may foster a deepening confidential relationship.

When Hard Work and Competence Are Not Enough

MURIEL D. WHORLEY

I N TODAY'S SOCIETY IT appears that we are motivated from early childhood by money. When you're a toddler, you're handed a dollar when your uncle or aunt comes to visit. After a while, it is no longer enough that they came to visit, it is practically an expectation that they give you something either when they arrive or when they leave. The money may say, "I am glad to see you" or "I value you" or any other combination. As you mature, you're handed an allowance. The money may say, "Here's your reward for doing your chores" or "I know you need this to survive amongst your peers" or, once again, any combination. You mature a little more and you get an after school job. The paycheck says, "This is what you get for what you gave." You begin to believe "if I do more than I'll get more." Next you ponder, "hmm, how can I get more?" More factors come into play, "I need additional education" "I can work more hours" or "I need a marketable skill." But the result is the same—if I give more—I'll get more.

But as you narrow down your choices—your choices become more clearly defined. For example, I don't want to work any more hours than I am working now, therefore, I need a more marketable skill or I need higher education. So you choose less hours, therefore you choose an alternate path, e.g. perhaps higher education. Higher education in today's environment means—college or graduate school. Now your choices are more clearly focused: What is my goal? Which school will get me there? Do I have what it takes to get accepted into this school?

Do I have the financial resources needed? AND, I need to graduate with a competitive edge.

OR, I need to hone my natural skills to compete in today's environment. I may be a natural athlete and would consider using that talent to get me financially situated. But what if I sustain an injury—what is plan B? You may be a writer, a carpenter, a painter, etc. and would consider a trade school or a school that specializes in the arts. Same scenario, what do you need to do to come out with a competitive edge? Competition is very real—it all comes down to this: your goal is to be financially solvent at all times. You don't want to struggle, to scrimp or to do without. You want to be able to help yourself, your family and your loved ones. It's as simple as that. You want to be, in *today's terms*, "A Success" which is unfortunately spelled M-O-N-E-Y.

Whichever path you choose, you're ultimately driven by the desire to succeed. After you have completed the requirements to rise above the competition and land the opportunity of a lifetime, you feel that the hard part is behind you and once you prove yourself to your organization, the road to success is inevitable. After all "HARD WORK AND COMPETENCE SHOULD BE THE KEY"—right?

However, is it really? Or do other factors come into play? Once you take into consideration the rational aspects of this scenario, the inevitable answer is: I have the right skills + I am self-motivated and willing to go above and beyond to get the job done = I will prove myself and I will succeed.

But what you have failed to realize is that there is a human aspect that is thrown into the equation. There are some who recognize your potential, don't want you to succeed and will place a plethora of stumbling blocks in your path. The key to your success is to remain vigilant about the task, your desire to be successful, and the ultimate goal which is to get the job done right, and on or before time. This is not easy because you are never sure of what the obstacles will be, where they will be or what form they will take. In fact, you may initially be unaware that there will be unknown external obstacles which you will face. There may be family issues that surface that need your attention and take you away from the task at hand. You may face an unexpected illness that requires a long absence from the job. The fact is there are eventualities that you will face that you were not prepared for and will surely undermine your efforts and your hard work. But when does it become "not enough?"

It becomes "not enough" when you allow the challenges to overcome you, to bewilder you, and to make you less than you know you can be. It becomes "not enough" when you say to yourself and to others "This is an impossible task and I can't do it"; instead of "this is an opportunity to rise above this challenge and I am determined to do it." It becomes "not enough" when you take your eye away from the ultimate goal of accomplishment and place it firmly on the overwhelming obstacles that have been placed in your path.

I have been there. I, too, knew that I had the skills needed to get the job done, was motivated to succeed, had a strong desire to accomplish— make my mark, and I knew what I was doing, was politically savvy and heavily invested in the result. I was caught totally unaware and I initially faltered. Did I mention that a supporter within the organization can also be a major key to your success because they keep you motivated to succeed? That's what helped me.

I was placed in a position of being the right hand to the highest executive in that organization. What I didn't realize, didn't expect, and didn't understand was that my competency never came into question, my culture did. Top executives at the highest level of the organization did not want or value African-Americans in any position of authority. There was such intensity that the desire to get me out of the position superseded the goal of getting the job done. That was an eye-opener for me. I knew that racism and bigotry existed; I just thought we had risen above it for the ultimate good. The more I was targeted, the harder I worked, the longer hours I put in because I wanted to prove to them I was a valued employee. Big mistake, I didn't need to prove it to them; I couldn't prove it to them; they didn't want to know it; they would never value me or any contributions I made, and the more I succeeded, the more obstacles they ensured I faced. I had organizational supporters that continuously reminded me of my value and that working longer hours and working harder and harder was not the answer. The answer was in the realization that I would never please that group of people and that it didn't matter how much I did, how much I accomplished—it would never be enough. I didn't realize it then but I am here to tell you that I realize it now. I would never be good enough for them, so why was I trying to—I had set me an impossible task.

What I should have done was recognize that I was a valuable asset who was making an effective contribution and let my accomplishments stand on their own merit. The hardest part of a scenario such as this is recognition—recognizing that you will never please everyone but you should at least complete the task at hand, timely, accurately, and with integrity. Believe me—that is the key when "*hard work and competence*" don't appear to be enough—they really are enough, the key is in knowing.

When Your Expertise and Seniority Work Against You

MURIEL D. WHORLEY

ONE OF THE TOUGHEST challenges African-Americans face in the workplace is having a manager who doesn't have the level of qualifying experiences or expertise as you. It is a constant internal struggle to balance respecting the position of your manager to make the decision vs. accepting a decision you know isn't right and not being true to your ethical values and to yourself. We have worked for so long to "earn" our place in society that it is incomprehensible that we have to earn that place daily.

I have personally been provided with the opportunity and overcame the challenges in order to excel in many positions. I have helped to design, develop, and implement organizations. I have effectively marketed organizations. I have made critical decisions that have positively impacted organizations, yet I find that based upon my culture, I am continuously placed in subordinate positions to executives that have less seniority and expertise than me.

Remember I mentioned the internal struggle—it is very real. It can impact you physically, mentally, and emotionally, if you don't take charge of you. You can't change the external factors. It is quite evident that, in today's environment, we are faced with situations that we cannot change. Oftentimes reason does not come into play. It boils down to this—when you are in charge—you write the ticket. Now, let's dissect this—what can you do? You can stay or you can leave. Simple. You do have options, they may not be the options you would have chosen for yourself but they exist. You can exist or you can survive. You can give in or you can fight. The only constant is you can impact you.

As leaders we have the desire to make an impact. It is impossible for true leaders to sit back and watch things happen. We have an internal drive that compels us to analyze and overcome odds. That's why we seek positions that are stressful and challenging. We have an overwhelming desire to beat the odds and come out on top. Therefore, when we are placed in a subordinate position and we have the seniority and expertise, while others don't, we have a burning desire to excel. Don't get me wrong, there are many ways to accomplish this goal. The key is in finding the right way. You can hold others up to ridicule, but showing up their ignorance will do nothing more than earn you a seat on the sidelines, or you can work in concert and bring others along with you. It's all in the presentation.

Unfortunately people are often not receptive when they are leading you. If I am your leader, naturally I know more, am more competent and bring more expertise. True leaders don't believe this. True leaders believe that it takes teamwork to accomplish a goal and they are not afraid of someone having more expertise than they. They welcome it.

But let's focus on the few that do. I have had leaders who make it a personal goal and their life's ambition to harm anyone they perceive can expose their vulnerabilities. They lash out, they sabotage, they seek to destroy. What does that look like? They create a hostile working environment with constant criticisms and unnecessary comparisons of work products and other innuendos. They lead by fear. They wreak what I call "mind havoc." They are determined to undermine your value by getting you to believe you are not valuable. They are ruthless and determined and quite often they are successful. Why? Because **you** give in and **you** give up. They eliminate your support network. They divide and conquer. And they are good. They elevate themselves by making you appear less expert than you are. They then come in and save the day. They are organizational bullies and they are in leadership positions. What did you do wrong? Nothing, you merely exposed their lack of leadership abilities, their lack of technical astuteness, and you embarrassed them. You have to pay. That payment is in the form of destroying your reputation and your career—all because you had an expertise that was lacking in them.

Now—what can you do? You can play the game with them—but it starts with you. And listen close, because this is not easy. You cannot let them undermine your confidence in you. You cannot become flustered and make apparent mistakes. You form an alliance with others and you work cohesively to impact the environment. This may take the form of an underground railroad. You don't expose *YOUR* vulnerabilities, and we all have them. You don't iterate theirs—the blame game is never an effective tool for true leaders. You own up to your mistakes and you learn by them. You are patient and you are thorough. You are never seen disparaging others. You are never critical. You are the consummate professional and you are an expert. You let your actions speak for you and your work products work for you. You are firm. You are confident. You let others extol your virtues because others are extolling their vices. You don't place yourself in a position where others see your vices—we all have them. But you don't bury your mistakes— you freely admit them and what actions you took to ensure they won't happen again. In other words, we value ourselves and others will value us. To accomplish this will not be easy and you will falter. I have, and I am not proud of it but it is with pride that I freely admit to the mistake of allowing a toxic environment to sway me from my value of never undermining others. I encourage you to lead by example. Let your emotional intelligence lead the way.

Managerial and
Executive Self-Destruction

■

PETER CHARLES

HAVE YOU EVER WATCHED someone who just seems to have everything going on? I am referring to that person who exudes confidence and appears on a clear path to galactic stardom. Many of us have. Here are a few questions to ask about these rising stars and perhaps the most critical question is, does power corrupt? A cliché, but what does it really do? *Power* is defined as the ability to control others; authority; sway; and influence. *Corrupt* is defined as changed from a sound condition to an unsound one. Each of us knows of at least one example of ruin by someone that can be traced to the power vested in that individual. How do you recognize when you have set yourself up for failure and self-destruction?

Let us examine the case of Jonathan Talbot. Jonathan is a senior manager in a large public relations firm with a reputation as an "employer of choice." Jonathan has climbed the corporate ladder through hard work and tenacity. He is single, handsome, charming, articulate and respected by his employees, peers and superiors alike. He is viewed by most as demanding but fair and a golden boy with a bright future. In fact, senior partners of the firm have discussed Jonathan's viability to succeed the senior vice president of his division. Jonathan manages a staff of thirty marketing and advertising professionals. His ambition leaves little room for socializing and he usually works 16-hour days, often sleeping in his office.

Because of his work regimen, Jonathan regularly complains to his secretary and staff assistant that he is barely able to manage the most basic chores of his personal life, such as laundering, shopping and maintaining his home and automobile. Jonathan's staff is sympathetic to his dilemma and wants to see him succeed. After all, they know Jonathan enjoys an excellent reputation within the company and they want to ride his coattails to a potentially more lucrative position. They are vying for a newly created executive assistant position within the division and are counting on his support.

Sara Marshall is Jonathan's secretary. She is a recent graduate with a Master's degree from a well-known business school and took this position while she contemplated her future. Sara is quiet, studious, and pretty. She is also ambitious, but until recently she was uncertain of the line of business she wanted to pursue. Sara decided that she enjoys public relations work and believes she has the acumen and demonstrated capability to be very successful in marketing. She has mapped a career path out of the secretarial and into the managerial ranks. She views attaining the executive assistant position as the first step toward reaching her goals. Sara solicits and receives Jonathan's counsel and support as a candidate for the position.

Sheila Stevens is Jonathan's staff assistant. She has been with the company and working under Jonathan for five years. Sheila graduated from a local university with a degree in commercial art. She was secretary to Jonathan before she was promoted to the position of staff assistant. Sheila is competent in her job, attractive, vivacious and well-liked by everyone. She is also ambitious and has longed to advance to a senior position in advertising. Jonathan supported Sheila for the staff assistant position and has frequently provided career counseling to her throughout the years. They have mapped out a time table for Sheila's development and Jonathan is fully cognizant of her ambitions and that she covets the executive assistant position because it demonstrates a logical progression toward realizing her aspirations.

Jonathan, Sara, and Sheila are planning a grueling schedule for Jonathan in the weeks and months to come. Jonathan comments that he hasn't any idea how he will get through the period. He has a growing and equally demanding social calendar that includes serving as the best man at his brother's wedding. Sara and Sheila volunteer to help Jonathan through the dilemma by doing whatever errands are necessary to prepare Jonathan for his brother's wedding. They comment that they can accomplish many of the tasks Jonathan is required to undertake for his brother's wedding during business hours. This includes scheduling and planning a bachelor party.

Jonathan appreciates the offer, but knows instinctively that he should decline and manage on his own. The offer, he feels, would represent an inappropriate use of company resources and may be negatively perceived by others. Up until now, his judgment has served him well. However, Jonathan is growing more and more concerned about the demands on his time and the pressure is beginning to affect his productivity. For their part, Sara and Sheila genuinely want to help Jonathan, but recognize that any business failure by Jonathan could reflect poorly on them at a critical juncture in their careers.

What would you do, if you were Jonathan?

Sara and Sheila continue to cajole Jonathan, offering their perspectives on how well they could help him manage his obligations to his brother. Jonathan knows their assistance in his personal matters would help him focus on his professional responsibilities. After all, he thinks, it would be for a short period of time until I am through this critical period of business demands. He reasons that his impeccable reputation in the company would carry him in the event anyone questioned the temporary arrangement with his secretary and staff assistant. Jonathan accepts the help. He focuses on his work and by all accounts everything goes off without a hitch at his brother's bachelor party. This thanks to as many as 3 – 4 hours a day spent by each Sara and Sheila in the office or running errands planning the party. They even serve as hostesses during the event.

What problems do you see with this scenario?

In the meantime, the selection committee for the executive assistant position had narrowed a large field of candidates to five and was preparing for final interviews. Sara and Sheila were among the finalists. The day before the interviews were scheduled to take place, the company's president was alerted by counsel that an anonymous complaint was lodged against the company for unfair and biased employment practices. The complaint cited favoritism and chronicled the activities of Jonathan, Sara and Sheila over the past few months and detailed the use of company resources for personal gain. The complaint also alleged a romantic and sexual involvement among the trio suggesting a virtual orgy at Jonathan's brother's bachelor party. The complaint threatened to go public with the intent of undermining the company's reputation should either Sara or Sheila land the executive assistant position. Further activity of the selection committee was suspended.

Jonathan, Sara and Sheila each were interviewed about their activities. They were forthcoming about the events and circumstances of the past few months proclaiming no intent to harm the company, but rather to ensure the successful realization of business objectives. Each acknowledged poor judgment concerning the bachelor party. Jonathan assumed complete responsibility for the actions of the three, particularly for permitting perceptions to grow that were harmful to the company name. He was fired. Sara and Sheila were reassigned.

What lessons can be learned from this case?

The Challenges of Geographical Mobility

HENRY O. LAMAR, JR.

R EGARDLESS OF THE AMOUNT that has been written or spoken about it, mention mobility (the act of relocating from one city or state to another) and you will still get a heated reaction from people most affected by it. Managers and executives in my agency knew that mobility was necessary to keep fresh perspectives and new ideas in the organization.

On the other hand, families and others who have moved know the hardships associated with moving. This article is about my family's experiences based on 11 relocations during my career.

The relocations began when I moved from Macon to Atlanta, GA to assume a position as an administrative intern on June 7, 1971. I was married soon after on June 27, 1971 and my wife joined me in Atlanta. Our first challenge was leaving our parents and other strong ties in Macon. Relocating encompasses many of life's most stressful events. Nobody likes the thought of leaving family and friends behind, yanking the kids out of school or asking a spouse to give up a perfectly good job. My wife and I had attended the same elementary school, become high school sweethearts and eventually graduated from the same college, 22 miles south of Macon. We had established significant roots, but we also realized that in order to give ourselves the chance to build our own lives, we had to explore opportunities outside of our hometown and outside of the arc of safety provided by family and friends.

Life changes the moment you decide to relocate, and it often takes several months to completely settle and feel "at home" in your new surroundings. Relocating is an often overwhelming experience that draws upon physical and emotional resources. Physical resources include energy expended cleaning the home being relocated from, making repairs to walls (particularly where pictures or plaques have been removed), removing window treatments and other items that will not remain in the home to be sold, packing clothing and other personal items (computers, games, school supplies, etc.) for use in temporary quarters (if necessary), packing paperwork (financial, medical, etc.) for use in the home loan application process in the new area and enrolling children in new schools, and loading items in vehicles you will be traveling in. Emotional resources include energy expended severing ties with family, friends, neighbors, schools, churches, community organizations, and jobs. Facing these changes will require the entire family to adjust. You'll become more sensitive to and appreciative of the kindnesses of friends, family, and others who help you along the way.

We remained in Atlanta for six years, during which time many wonderful things happened for us, including the birth of our son in 1973. At the time of his birth, relocating to another city was not even on my mind. My goal was to support my wife and child as well as possible where we resided at the time. Little did I know at the time that I would become ambitious and, in order to progress in my agency, need to move to other locations to gain additional experience. I made the decision that in order to gain additional work experience in the organization, I would make myself available not only for a promotion, but a change to a lower grade or a reassignment.

While I felt total responsibility for supporting my family, my wife was also working in Atlanta and our son was adjusting well in his new daycare. Relocating was not a decision that I could make alone. I talked with my wife about my feelings and about the financial opportunities that relocating could bring to our family. My wife was very supportive of my aspirations and indicated that we would deal with problems together. While this was a life-defining moment for us, it was only the first such discussion that we would have over time.

My family and I relocated from Atlanta to Columbia, South Carolina in 1977. This was the beginning of many challenges we had to face as a family. While I was changing jobs, I was at least with the same company.

My wife had to start over in the new location and our son had to adjust to a new school. Remember, your positive attitude about relocating does not necessarily make your child or spouse more receptive to this sudden change and confusion. By this I mean that while they may share your excitement about career enhancement and financial rewards, they may not be so excited about being uprooted. A child's unique personality and developmental age influence how well relocation is handled. The best way to prepare a little one for change is simply with extra attention and positive reassurance. When relocating, babies may sense change as their schedules get disrupted. Older babies often fuss when encountering many new people. Some teens see moving as an opportunity to get a fresh start with schools, friends or even family. Others are very reluctant to leave relationships that they've established. They may express fear or anger at the thought of loneliness. Teens who have moved many times often feel the most threatened at the thought of moving again. What your teenager says and doesn't say tells you a lot about feelings held inside. Sometimes true feelings are not shared because teens do not want to be viewed as being a hindrance to their parents' success. Sometimes when they do talk about relocating, they talk about what they see as positives for themselves or about what they think you want to hear. Although teens often communicate on an adult level about certain issues, they still need extra love and support. Encourage open conversation, no matter what the topic. Share details of the relocation with children and your spouse so they feel included. Taking the mystery out of relocating will often ease their fears. The comfort of familiar routines helps make the relocation less stressful. My wife would always decorate our son's room in our new home as similarly as possible to what his previous room looked like. This helped him to adjust to the new home environment fairly quickly. As a result, my wife and I adjusted more quickly.

In 1979, we relocated from Columbia, South Carolina to Pelham, Alabama, a town just south of Birmingham. This move brought on additional stress for all of us. In addition to the normal stress of relocating, we also had to deal with late night harassment in our new neighborhood. Individuals would "trench" our yard by driving vehicles through it. They also placed toilet paper on our trees and shrubs. Our neighbors were shocked at the "trenching," but told us that the papering was just a prank by neighborhood kids. The kids allegedly did that to the homes of people that they liked. We didn't think so. After a few nights of this activity, I filed a discrimination complaint with the Department of Justice. Subsequently, federal officials visited a few homes in our neighborhood and the activity stopped. I later found out that the ringleaders of the harassment were the teenage sons of our next-door neighbors.

In 1983, I was selected for a position in Memphis, Tennessee. This was the first time that I had to leave my family behind while I began work in a new city. I commuted from Pelham to Memphis for four months. It was important to our family that I spend as much weekend time with them as possible. So, I would leave Pelham at 2:00 a.m. every Monday morning and drive four hours to Memphis to begin work by 7:30 a.m. The commute was necessary because it took us four months to sell our home in Pelham. This was prior to authorization for the use of relocation service contracts, including the home purchase option where a contractor would make an offer to purchase your home. You had 30 days to consider the offer and either accept it or reject it. If the offer was not accepted, you continued to try to sell your home through the normal real estate process. This could take a long time. My wife was working in Birmingham and our son had begun elementary school. My wife's job, her responsibility for transporting our son to and from school as well as maintaining our home, added to the burden of our four-month separation.

We later relocated from Memphis to Centreville, Virginia in 1987. The relocation to Virginia required us to purchase a home for double the amount that we sold for in Memphis and with less square footage. Again, my wife had to start over in her career. She was not able to transfer from one job to another with the same company as I could. She had to start the job seeking process from the beginning each time we relocated. Our son had to change schools in the middle of the school year. We moved back to Atlanta in 1989. This was one of our most challenging relocations because our son was in the middle of his junior year in high school and was flourishing as an athlete and student leader. Despite that significant challenge, we all were excited about the opportunity to relocate near our hometown. We were excited about being near our parents and other relatives. Our excitement in that regard was short-lived. My mother passed away within a month after we relocated. My wife's mother passed away within the year.

Once again, my wife had to change jobs. Our son had to change schools and make new friends again. Thank God, neither of them ever said "Hell no, I won't go." Without their love, support, and understanding, I could not have maintained my sanity as well as my family. My wife took on new jobs and flourished in them. Our son made easy relocation adjustments despite the significant impact they had on him. The most difficult relocation for him was when we relocated during his junior year in high school. Before we relocated, he had been a starter on his football team and had been voted president of his upcoming senior class. After we relocated to Atlanta, and enrolled him in school, we were amazed at how well he transitioned. Staying involved in sports helped him tremendously. He made the football team at his new school and they won the state high school championship in his senior year.

If that had been me in high school, I don't know how I would have reacted to having to move from one school to another, let alone from one high school to another. My circumstances, however, were totally different. My father did not have the kind of job that required his family to move from state to state or city to city. I never had to make the kind of adjustments that my wife and son had to make in support of me. I kept that fact in the forefront of my mind as I tried to cope with the adjustments my wife and son experienced.

In 1991, my wife and I relocated to Cincinnati, Ohio and left our son behind at college in Atlanta. We, in essence, became "empty nesters" at that point. That was a very difficult time for all of us. My wife and I didn't have our son at home or near home and had to adjust to the lack of activities that had been associated with him in the past. We also had to adjust to having more time available to ourselves. Our son began the challenging, but necessary transition from having mom and dad nearby for advice, to dealing with more issues on his own. From Cincinnati, my wife and I relocated to Cleveland, Ohio in 1993, from there to Jacksonville, Florida in 1995, from there to Germantown, Maryland in 1999, and from there back to Atlanta in 2003.

Each relocation resulted in enhancements to my career, but at great expense to my wife and son. The three of us developed a very strong support system which helped to conquer the challenges we faced. While many relocations and the accompanying challenges caused stress over the years, we were able to face the challenges because of the strength of our relationship. We grew as a family unit from those challenges, and despite the issues we faced, we are glad that we had the opportunity to experience different people and different places during our lives.

The transitions were not easy, but from them, we learned many valuable lessons. Whether it's your first relocation from home, a retirement relocation, or any relocation in between, planning can seem overwhelming. The relocating has to fit into all the other things you do in life that are already stressful. If you are young and single, the thought of relocating may be exciting, but it can also make you nervous about new friends, a new job, or new expenses. Perhaps you or your spouse are relocating because of a new job and are worried about what effects the relocation will have on your family. Just remember, concerns about the unknowns are typical, even if you've relocated many times before. Regardless of your situation, if you are prepared with some essential tips, your family can experience a healthy adjustment.

Following are some tips to remember:

Plan

Whenever possible, plan a trip to your new destination. Whether you're house-hunting or just taking a drive around your new neighborhood, a pre-planning trip can help make the adjustment for children a lot easier. Familiarity can be a source of confidence.

Communicate

Share what you feel with the others involved – both the issues that excite you as well as those that make you nervous or apprehensive. Communicating your feelings can relieve stress and boost your self-confidence.

Don't Neglect Your Health

In between running around and getting organized, take time to eat well, get plenty of sleep and exercise. This can help you stay healthy, both physically and psychologically.

Stay in Touch

A friendly, familiar voice is just a phone call away when you feel overwhelmed. Talking with someone who understands you oftentimes helps to alleviate stress, allowing you to relax. I traveled extensively during my career. I made a point to call home every night that I was on the road. This helped my psyche as well as helped me to be in touch with what was happening with my family during our separation.

Build a Foundation

Try to form new relationships without draining your emotions. There are plenty of activities in which to get involved – get involved in school functions or become active in your neighborhood or local civic and religious organizations. Getting involved as early as possible helps you to relax and cope with the stress of the relocation.

Don't Expect an Immediate Adjustment

Expecting your new life to immediately "click" can be frustrating. You have to adapt to new surroundings and discover the features of your new community. With a little time you'll feel right at home.

Get Settled

Getting settled means getting comfortable with your new surroundings. Getting unpacked and organizing your new home generates feelings of relief as well as feelings of normality. Once the physical unpacking is done, however, there's still the personal adjustment to make. Growing comfortable emotionally can take time, so don't be surprised by some bumps in the road. Even the closest families can experience a significant adjustment period before finally feeling "'at home."

If you think your relocation has affected you or a family member for the worse, don't put off seeking professional counseling. Just as you see a doctor for a physical exam, getting a personal check-up with a counselor can help ease an adjustment to new surroundings. To stay physically and personally healthy, it's a good idea to see someone before stress gets the better of you.

Relocation is not just about people changing jobs, it's also about changing their lives. Despite the fact that the relocation is different for different people, individuals tend to be more willing to relocate when they are young and before the onset of family responsibilities. The desire for stability tends to increase with age. I was happy to move around, but as I got older and my family grew around me, it definitely became harder to do, not just with regard to my job, but also as a husband and father.

Remember, although it opens up a world of opportunities for you, your family, and your future, relocating can be a challenge. We can't ever know exactly what lies on the road ahead – the best advice is to be prepared for the unexpected.

Executive Level Member of the "Club" With Various Levels of Membership

JAMES E. ROGERS, JR. ESQ

THERE IS A COMMON misconception that if a person and/or group reaches a certain achievement in their lives and/or careers that this achievement conveys equal status, equal opportunities for success and equal benefits. Nothing could be further from the truth. This common misconception presents itself in society and in the workplace.

One does not have to make a concerted effort to find evidence of the misconception. Clearly the nation's experience regarding Hurricane Katrina demonstrates this point. The world watched in horror as thousands of people were displaced from their homes and businesses because of the devastation resulting not only from the hurricane along the Gulf Coast, but also from the breach of the levies protecting New Orleans. The world watched as the local, state, and federal governments failed our fellow citizens. Beyond the human suffering, loss of life, and the immeasurable economic and societal impact of the event, the new "status" of the displaced population added to the level of anguish. Massive news coverage on television, radio, the Internet, and printed press labeled the displaced population as "refugees." How could U.S. citizens be labeled as refugees? The common definition of a refugee is one who flees to a foreign country or power to escape danger or persecution. Therefore regardless of race, color, wealth, or professional careers, the new status was "refugee."

This new status was promoted by the press and various national, state, and local leaders until a public outcry demanded a change in the status of the displaced population. The outcry was simply that U.S. citizens do not lose or change the status of their citizenship because of a natural disaster. However, a number of the displaced population who already had doubts as to their status in our society had their worst doubts confirmed. Thus it appears that although you may be a U.S. citizen, your citizenship may be of a different level than another.

So you ask what does this have to do with being an executive. A lot! The number of misconceptions of executive status and what it is and what it conveys is unlimited. Below we will discuss these misconceptions and provide tools to maintain your focus.

For the sake of discussion let's take a look at Kim, an African-American woman, who has been promoted as a new executive with XYZ corp. Kim has had an outstanding career with the company. She started with the company as an intern in college and after graduation began her career full time. After being groomed in a number of positions to enhance her skills she began her management career and excelled through the company's various levels of management. This included several moves around the country recommended by her mentors to expand her experience base. Now she has just been selected as an executive in the headquarters office and is beginning to experience forces and influences she did not expect.

Kim notices that everyone treats her differently than they did before this promotion. Being in and out of the headquarters for years working on different projects she was not an unknown commodity. She believed that she had developed friendships that would help her career and she could help her friends. However, after the announcement of her selection was made she noticed that some of her friends did not contact her to convey their congratulations. She also noted that she received well wishes from people that she had seen in meetings and in the hallways that previously would not speak to her unless put in the position whereby they had to. Various executives pledged their support, invited her to lunch, and offered loads of advice. She experienced a brief period of overwhelming popularity with executives and managers she did not know.

Kim was asked to attend different functions with her "new friends," but was discouraged from bringing her "old friends" along. She was told that they were not executives, and would not fit in. Further Kim was told that since she had arrived at another level in the organization she should limit her interaction with her "old" associates. She felt that there was a conscious effort being made to change her, to make her fit a certain stereotype. This was in addition to being given unreasonable stretch goals for her organization. She found that she did not get the "corporate support" needed to reach the organizational goals. She further found that all of her decisions and actions were questioned and second guessed, initially privately and later publicly, by her new friends. With all of the professional changes in her life Kim became frustrated and felt isolated. She began having health problems and began to engage in self destructive behavior. A combination of these things led to the end of a promising career with XYZ corp.

Kim's experience is not unique. This scenario is repeated again and again in our society and in the workplace.

The common misconception is that if you have made it to the executive level you have it "made" but that is not the case. There are a number of factors that impacted Kim of which she may not have been aware. Below we will discuss some of these factors.

Although Kim may have had a number of experiences with the corporation prior to her selection she may not have known various factors impacting her selection. For example, was she selected on her merit solely, but also because she was female and African-American? Was the fact that she was female and African-American important because of outside pressures as in lawsuits, discrimination complaints, or the need for more diversity to get business? Further, who were her primary competitors, and who were their friends and allies, and what impact did they have on Kim's operation? The bottom line is whether the organization intended Kim to be successful. Key players at the executive level may have put things in motion that may have impacted that determination before she took on her new role.

Most organizations have various executive levels. The organizational chart may give insight, however; the "power levels" are generally not on the organizational chart.

The executive "club" is determined by friendship, historical relationships, power, and influence, not status; and that "club" has various levels of membership. To assure success you must be keenly aware of these factors, always be vigilant, utilize due diligence, and be aware that club levels have a price.

This process may frighten some and make others very apprehensive, however; I assure you that these factors can be successfully navigated toward a very promising and rewarding career and life. Some of my suggestions may appear simple, but I have found that most complicated situations become overwhelming when individuals and organization fail to look for the simple solutions first!

The first element is to know yourself extremely well. What **is** your history and the history of your family? These are very important in determining your own self-worth and self-value. If you and/or your family members have had to overcome overwhelming challenges and great opposition then you can easily rely on your own "history of victory" as a foundation for taking on new challenges. These victories should not be taken lightly, simply because, since the beginning of time, human nature has not changed. What you have experienced on the street, in school, and in various organizations is simply repeated at another level. All people will not like or support you! There are "haters" — those who hate you for being successful, and those who will hate you because *they* are not. These "haters" will use various forms of discrimination to redefine and reduce your credibility including race, sex, age, religion, social status, whether you attended private schools, etc., to halt and/or delay your progress and create obstacles. Any obstacle has the potential to be effective, but the only effective obstacle is one you give power. Most effective obstacles are those that cause you to question yourself and your abilities and distract you from your goals. The key is that most of the "club members" who hope to control you will not directly attack you to destroy you; the effective process is to distract you from your goal and/ or focus, and then watch you expend energy and effort in meaningless activities. This is in addition to the organizational and cultural landmines that may not be fatal at first violation, but the cumulative effect may be.

I cannot overemphasize the importance of knowing yourself and your values. Everything in life has a price and knowing yourself is key in determining your options. The scriptures are very clear in asking the question, what does it mean to gain the world and lose your soul? Knowing yourself will guide you in making these decisions that, at night, will allow you to look at yourself in the mirror, or look your spouse and/

or children in the eye and know that you have been true to yourself. This empowers you to maintain *CONTROL* of your life and career. When you give in to the schemes of the "club," you allow the "club" to define you, and, you give up control. Personal control enhances the opportunities for you to select options and your choice of options will lead to your success.

Often I'm asked why is knowing yourself and having a strong foundation regarding your values and principles so important. The answer is because at the executive level every fiber of your being *will* be tested. Some of these tests are put in place to test the strength of your convictions. Others are presented to unethically gain wealth and power for the corporation and/or executive "club" members. Based on recent criminal charges and convictions of key "club" members of corporations and businesses across the country, one can only wonder whose values and principles were tested, and if their criminal activity was contrary to their values and principles, why did they fail the test? Or maybe they were so immersed in immoral activity that they could not tell what was wrong from what was acceptable.

The decisions may be tough but the solutions are easy. BE TRUE TO YOURSELF. Because at the end of the day you only have you, your family and close friends and they are all that matter. Do not get yourself in the box that the current executive position is all that is available to you. Keep your options open, keep control, and move if the need arises to a position that fits your principles, goals, and aspirations. If your skills have moved you up to the "club level" in your current organization, the same skills will help you achieve similar heights in another organization.

Education is the second simple solution. Again, you ask why education? Knowledge is a great equalizer in corporations and society. Degrees from accredited institutions may add the appearance of credibility to your status. Although you are generally surrounded by others with degrees and various accomplishments, if you happen to be female and/or a minority your peers may find your presence intimidating. If they are intimated this may be your "edge" in many situations. Many may approach you to attempt to make you conform or try to make you fit in by their standards. DON'T DO IT! Never convey weakness, rather strength. Maintain the elements of your core values and personality that make you the person you are. God made you who He wanted you to be, and He made you first class. Therefore, don't devalue yourself to anyone.

Education also opens the door for ongoing learning. At the executive level it is critical that you maintain a system of learning that keeps you on the information forefront. This includes reading periodicals, taking online courses and seminars, and listening to books on tape, etc. Confidence is often displayed because you know your subject matter, many times better than your colleagues and/or competitors. This ongoing learning process will keep you fresh and on the cutting edge of new developments in your field of expertise. The additional learning and skill may help you find your niche in the organization and within your industry. Discovering your niche and expanding its impact may make you invaluable to the organization. This will not guarantee that your "haters" will not attempt to derail your career, however, the corporation will have to assess whether they want to incur the cost of losing your expertise and replacing it.

The key is to find a niche that enables the corporation to be successful by impacting its bottom line.

Going back to our friend Kim she did not get outside the "corporate box" to make herself invaluable. She let others define her and therefore limit her progress as well as the progress of those who were loyal and supportive of her. It is important that when we find ourselves in Kim's position that we return to the basic concepts of our foundation.

The third key is utilizing your resources. Resources are not limited to money or wealth. In fact by leveraging every aspect of what may be a resource you will find that your you have unlimited resources. I view resources as people and systems that can aid me in reaching my goals. Thus I leverage my money, my associations, friendships, and relationships. It is great to have the "hook-up." This is not to use people for self-gain, but to be an asset to those who help you and you pay it forward even to those who cannot help you. As you do so, the circle of your resources constantly expands.

Leveraging resources is not a process where you gain or sell at any price to achieve your goals. To the contrary it is your values that must be your guide. With your guide in place don't be afraid to ask for assistance from those persons or institutions that meet your criteria, while knowing that a reciprocal request may come to you. If the person or institution does not meet your criteria leave them alone. A possible short term gain is not worth long term complications and misunderstandings.

Networking is one of the key means of leveraging your resources. In my view the term networking is over utilized and improperly applied. Generally networking is described as an opportunity to meet different *people* at a reception or affair and pass and trade business cards. Some believe that the exchange of cards and a follow-up conversation or lunch means that you have effectively networked. I disagree with this concept. True networking goes several steps further. Not only do you exchange cards and have the follow-up conversation or meeting, but also you have to put into place the opportunity to serve the one you wish to network with.

Actively seek the opportunity to utilize your skill, talent, and/or expertise to benefit that person without seeking compensation. Seeking compensation conveys that you are only seeking a job opportunity. Networking may lead to compensation for both parties at a future point after a relationship has developed however true networking is the epitome of "*quid pro quo.*" In essence you provide help today to obtain help tomorrow. Further, if tomorrow never comes your posture is still improved. Networking is work. If someone does something for you, you must be prepared to return the service and/or provide similar support to those in the network that seek it. Networking at this level conveys instant credibility. This means if someone in your network makes a request and/or a referral and you make it happen, you are in the position to obtain future support.

The last two points go hand in hand. You have to have the intestinal fortitude (guts) to make it happen and the faith to believe it will. Many times in business, sports, and other endeavors you can tell who will win by the "swagger." The walk, the look of confidence and success are very formidable for most people, who believe it. Those that don't are just as insecure as you are. Therefore, to give yourself the edge regarding others in the "club" you must show that you have the fortitude to make wise choices and stick to them and/or be willing to change if the circumstances require that you do so. Being stubborn may not convey strength, but may convey stupidity. Practice the skill of being willing to change when circumstances require change, but be wise to maintain your position if the circumstance does not meet your standards. This skill requires that you have faith and trust in your abilities regardless of the "haters."

As you deal with the various levels of membership in the "club" keep in mind the five key points:

- Remember your history of victory
- Strive for your education and continual learning
- Develop your resources
- Utilize your intestinal fortitude (GUTS!)
- Enhance your faith

What to Do When You Are the Alleged Discriminating Official

PETER CHARLES

The obvious answer to the question of what to do when you are the alleged discriminating official is to know that you are innocent and that you have nothing to suggest that you are anything but beyond reproach. The reverse posture is to practice stupidity. And stupidity, unfortunately, is not at a premium for anyone.

From the subtle to the assiduous, the learned tendency for practicing discrimination against others for non-merit reasons permeates our society. It is contrary to every human being's subconscious sense that there are traits and differences to be studied, embraced and assimilated from each person we meet into the make-up and/or character of self. So, what is stupid or intolerable discrimination? It is the individual who, although aware of the consequences of his or her actions, cannot seem to control themselves from comments, actions or practices that set the stage for discrimination allegations.

Consider Carl. Despite his apparent but generally acceptable social indiscretions, he has managed to achieve supervisory status within a national union headquarters organization. Carl manages a mixed group of 15 support staff of varying races and ethnicities, including Asians, in the union's national headquarters. He has a blue collar background having worked the shipping docks of New Jersey for nearly 20 years. He has recently been promoted to his current position. He has been in this position for three years. While Carl's job proficiency is adequate, he is condescending and patronizing to staff with differing backgrounds than his own. This is a subject of much discussion among his workers, a distraction and it inhibits productivity. His disrespectful conduct with his employees prompts many to complain and several to seek employment elsewhere. Following one encounter between Carl and a subordinate, the employee resigns and applies for unemployment compensation. Unemployment compensation is denied.

The employee files a discrimination complaint and seeks retribution from the union. The case winds its way through the employment discrimination process and ultimately to the Equal Employment Opportunity Commission. A finding of discrimination and judgment is levied against the union. The employee is awarded lost wages and punitive damages. The union is found to have permitted a continuing hostile environment to exist. Carl is fired.

What if Carl is innocent? He is the pillar of the community and treats everyone equally. Our recommended course of action for Carl is to stand his ground. That is, be cooperative and forthcoming in the process. He should explain his actions and purpose in the matter for which he is alleged to have discriminated. Carl has no need to be defensive, but rather his explanations should be matter of fact. Besides, no one knows better than Carl the intended purpose of his comments. There is nothing to fear about the process, if your actions and/or comments are based on merit and without bias toward any group or individual.

Leadership

HENRY O. LAMAR, JR.

T HIS ARTICLE IS ABOUT leadership and the impact it has on delivery of products and services in any organization. Leaders at all levels impact the success of the organization. Leaders balance leading people, serving customers, managing programs and demonstrating technical credibility. As a leader, you must develop your own leadership philosophy. In this article, I will explore my leadership philosophy in a manner that I hope will encourage you to explore your own.

I believe in honest and open communication, getting employees engaged in work processes and working as a team. Communication is an integral part of leadership. Assist your employees in knowing where to find the information they need to effectively perform their responsibilities. And remember, a key component of effective communication is active listening. Your ability to communicate effectively will enhance your performance and contribute to the success of your employees. In order to inspire employees to work as a team, the leader must be perceived as a team player. While being a team player has many meanings, one of the most important is to appear to be interchangeable with other leaders near your organizational level. To quote a former leader of mine, leaders must be "fungible," i.e., able to utilize their leadership skills in any part of the organization. Narrow specializations are discouraged as you progress in the leadership ranks. Another important meaning of team play is putting in long hours at the office. This requires a certain amount of sheer physical energy, even though a great deal of this time is spent not in actual work but in social interactions—like reading and discussing work materials, taking coffee or smoke breaks, or having informal conversations. These interactions forge the social bonds that make real leadership work—that is, group work of various sorts—possible. You must participate in the interactions to be considered effective in your job. Teams assembled by managers who know and understand their workers' personalities operate with minimum conflict. Everyone has a specialty and a contribution to make to the group. Members know and play to one another's strengths. As the leader, once you know personal behavior styles, you can move beyond personalities and get to the issues at hand.

I expect to be visible in the work area. My objective is to unite various functions in the organization that I'm leading with common goals and a cooperative spirit. I solicit robust and continuous communication. I want to know the good as well as the bad. If my employees don't feel good about their jobs, the workload, leadership decisions, the color on the walls, or anything else that keeps them from doing their jobs in a quality manner and feeling valued as a result, I want to know about it. Maybe I can change the environment that is causing concern, maybe I can explain the situation so that people understand why we must do what we are doing, or maybe I can't do anything about the issue that has been raised. The point of the matter is I can't even begin to address an issue unless I hear about it from the affected people. The most effective and efficient way to hear what you need to hear is to implement a true "open door" policy. My door is always open for employees to come to me and for me to go to where they are.

Honesty must be a necessity in our jobs, but it should also be a source of pride. From my perspective, there are few problems that can't be solved if I have a truthful and fully developed account of them. I expect people to make occasional mistakes. My hope is that they will learn from the mistakes and enhance their productivity and service. As another of my former leaders said, "if you don't do anything wrong, it's usually because you didn't do anything." I expect employees to make sure that I know the real story. Another part of honesty is how I am reacted to as a leader. If I'm doing something wrong or not doing something that I should be doing, I expect to be told. I make mistakes also and I appreciate them being pointed out to me before they receive too large an audience.

I cannot demand respect for myself, I must earn it. However, I do expect my employees to respect each other as professionals and as human beings. I want them to remember that we are all looking down the same barrel and we don't need any enemies on the home team. We spend at least a third of our waking hours on the job together. As often as we have to face sometimes irate and adversarial customers, I encourage employees to make sure that coming to our office provides a safe and secure feeling.

I want employees to smile a lot. I want the job to be enjoyable and our times together fun. I want to have lots of stories to laugh about when we're all long retired. My biggest fear as a leader is that I will have employees who hate coming to work.

As a leader, the above expectations are the ones I set for my employees. I also provide information on things that employees should expect of me. Employees can expect me to listen and be supportive. Employees can expect me to be free with rewards for results. They can expect me to try to be fair in promotions, evaluations, details and assignments. They can expect me to reward those who do their jobs very well, and not hold anyone back because of a bias or emotion. Employees can expect me to be a main proponent of their individual development. I want all of my employees to be the best they can be at the jobs they hold. Potential and success depend on how well employees develop their particular skills with the opportunities available to them and their desire and determination to take advantage of those opportunities. Employees must objectively take stock of their assets and liabilities, their strengths and areas needing improvement, and the degree and nature of their commitment. They must say to themselves "if it is to be, it is up to me."

I believe that my job as a leader is to set goals, find resources in both capital and people and understand the business and its dynamics. This means being personally and deeply engaged in the business. I must understand the business, the people who conduct the day-to-day business and the environment we all are working in. With that knowledge, I must set the tone for the kind of environment we want to nurture. Aside from that, my job is basically to get out of the way.

With those leadership thoughts in mind, I want to provide some keys to effective leadership. Regardless of where our leadership philosophies may stand at this time, we are all capable of moving our leadership style closer to the ideal by:

- Developing a work climate that encourages trust, candor and open communication with a free sharing of work related information. How people talk to each other absolutely determines how well the organization will function.
- Adopting the belief that the best motivation is self-motivation and that if the proper climate and leadership are provided, most employees will want to be productive and efficient.
- Involving employees in problem solving and improvement planning when they are in a position to make a contribution.
- Listening to employees and trying to see merit in their needs.
- Setting clear goals and helping employees understand organizational objectives.
- Rearranging jobs to allow a greater degree of responsibility and self-direction.
- Recognizing that conflict between the needs of individuals and the organization are inevitable, but should be confronted openly using problem solving strategies.
- Using mistakes as a learning opportunity rather than concentrating on placing blame.
- Having high expectations of others while providing them support and encouragement in attaining their objectives.
- Providing recognition for superior performance.

I think you should consider how these suggestions relate to your role as a leader and to your personal leadership philosophy. I also think that you should evaluate the extent to which you agree or disagree with them.

Individuals in organizations rarely can be successful alone; typically, they must influence, lead, and coordinate their efforts with others in order to achieve their goals. Your leadership success rests in large part on your ability to create organizational relationships which facilitate cooperation, performance, productivity, and mutual job satisfaction. Your ability to create such facilitating relationships depends on how you manage your own behavior so that it has the maximum positive impact on those around you. The way in which you approach your leadership role directly affects your ability to create relationships that produce cooperation, performance, productivity, and mutual job satisfaction.

The degree to which you are able to create relationships that positively influence others is largely a function of your day-to-day leadership practices. It is not a function of your personality, what you think, or what your attitudes are; rather, it is a function of what you do in your day-to-day behavior as you carry out your role within the organization. Organizational effectiveness is directly dependent upon your leadership impact. Technical competence, by itself, is not sufficient for successful job performance. You must also possess the competence to create organizational relationships that will allow both you and others to be mutually successful in your respective roles.

I believe that leadership strength is on the decline in many organizations. Developing leaders, even in best practice companies, is far from a risk-free activity. Placing high potential managers in developmental "stretch" assignments entails significant risk to the organization as well as to the individual. The identification of those individuals who are likely to receive the greatest benefit from development initiatives becomes critical. As with any business investment, organizations need to carefully monitor the risk by thoroughly assessing each individual's current set of capabilities and taking steps to support the individual placed in developmental assignments.

The processes and procedures organizations use to determine their high potential managers and executives must be fair, objective, and inclusive of the diversity that exists in the world today. The meaning of managing diversity has expanded well beyond traditional notions of race and gender. Leaders need to demonstrate a high level of sensitivity to, and respect for, cultural differences of customers, suppliers, employees, and government bodies. Successfully managing diversity demands managing across cultures and employing a variety of management styles to leverage the skills of multiple generations in the workplace. Non-merit factors such as who are the leader's friends or who is recommended by the leader's friends (no matter how cleverly disguised) should not be a part of any process used to determine participants in developmental training programs. Knowledge, skills and abilities should be the determining factors. While I believe youth and enthusiasm in leadership positions is critical for long-term organizational survival, it is critical to balance your organizational makeup with the wisdom and experience of mature workers.

I believe that current and future business challenges will require leaders to demonstrate excellence in strategic thinking, change management, relationship building, and talent development. Personal traits, that if not addressed, pose obstacles to leaders' future career success include risk aversion, hesitancy to take necessary business risks, personal arrogance and insensitivity, overly controlling leadership style, and a reluctance to deal with difficult people issues.

To quote a former executive associate of mine, "there are three types of leaders-those who make things happen, those who watch things happen, and those who say, what happened?" Which type of leader are you?

The majority of us admire leaders who are honest, competent, forward looking, inspiring, and ultimately, credible. Does this statement describe you?

Author Biographies

Henry O. Lamar, Jr.

Henry is an honor graduate of Fort Valley State College, Fort Valley, Georgia where he earned a Bachelor's Degree in Education with a concentration in social science. He holds a Master's Degree in Public Administration from the University of Georgia. He began his federal career as an administrative intern in 1971 and became a Federal Executive in 1986.

He completed 34 years of service with the federal government. Of those years, 28 were spent in managerial positions and executive positions. He received numerous performance awards during his career, including two Presidential Rank Awards (1995 and 2001). These are the highest forms of performance recognition a federal employee can receive.

Since retirement, Henry has been serving as a management consultant with several national consulting firms.

James E. Rogers, Jr. ESQ

James (Jim) Rogers, Jr. ESQ is a "cum laude" graduate of Bluefield State College, Bluefield, West Virginia, and the recipient of the "Dean's Award" from the University of Toledo College of Law where he was the first African-American to serve on Law Review. He began his federal career as a litigator in 1979 and became a Federal Executive in 1992. In addition to numerous awards for his expertise, leadership, and public service he was selected by Ebony Magazine as one of the "50 Young Leaders of the Future," and is the recipient of the Public Service Award from the Center for Leadership Development. While serving on various local and national organizational boards, he has made numerous television and radio appearances. He is in demand as a leading motivational speaker to a wide range of audiences from high schools, universities and colleges, all community groups, as well as top corporations on the leadership challenges of the day.

Muriel D. Whorley

Muriel is currently the Chief, Talent Management Branch (TMB) in a major government agency. She leads an organization comprised of a manager and senior human capital program managers who develop and execute programs which prepare employees with demonstrated leadership skills for leadership positions. Inherent in the TMB organization are elements of workforce planning, knowledge management and the identification of mission critical occupation skills and competency gaps. Muriel's organization assists her agency's executive leadership in the pre-identification of successful future leaders.

Muriel has also served as Senior Technical Advisor, Senior Operations Advisor, Executive Assistant to the senior executive in two major divisions of her agency, Director Communications, Program Manager, Staff Advisor, Chief, Staffing and Classification, and Budget Analyst.

Muriel began her career in 1973 as a COOP student and continued working both part-time and full-time while she was attending Howard University. She has completed several leadership courses such as Leading Leaders; Advanced Leadership – Influencing Outcomes; and an in-depth communications curriculum from the University of South Carolina. She is a member of the Professional Managers Association, The Society of Human Resources Managers, and the National Association of Professional Women.

Peter Charles

Peter Charles is the Chief Human Capital Officer in a cabinet level agency leading one of the Obama administration's major agenda initiatives.

He joined the agency in 2009. Prior to this appointment, he was senior advisor to the leader of one of the largest bureaus in another department and held the position of Human Capital Officer from 2006 to 2009. Among his varied positions with this organization, Peter served as the principal steward for human capital and human resources services. His focus was and continues to be on a full spectrum of human capital planning and HR operations, including learning and education, labor/management relations, and HR information services as well as strategic planning and development.

Peter's other federal experiences include appointments with the Department of Defense, where he directed local and agency-wide labor/employee relations, corporate recruiting, staffing, and classification programs. In his current role, he is principal advisor on human capital issues.

Peter is among a select group of federal senior executives to receive the Presidential Meritorious Rank award in 2006. He holds a Bachelor of Science Degree from Bowie State University and has completed graduate work at American University and the Catholic University of America.